The Roaring Twenties
and
Great Depression

By
CINDY BARDEN

COPYRIGHT © 2002 Mark Twain Media, Inc.

ISBN 1-58037-211-2

Printing No. CD-1557

Mark Twain Media, Inc., Publishers
Distributed by Carson-Dellosa Publishing Company, Inc.

Table of Contents

About the American History Series

Welcome to *The Roaring Twenties and Great Depression,* one of the books in the Mark Twain Media, Inc., American History series for students in grades four to seven.

The activity books in this series are designed as stand-alone material for classrooms and home-schoolers or as supplemental material to enhance your history curriculum. Students can be encouraged to use the books as independent study units to improve their understanding of historical events and people.

Each book provides challenging activities that enable students to explore history, geography, and social studies topics. The activities provide research opportunities and promote critical reading, thinking, and writing skills. As students learn about the people and events that influenced history, they will draw conclusions; write opinions; compare and contrast historical events, people, and places; analyze cause and effect; and improve thinking skills. Students will also have the opportunity to apply what they learn to their own lives through reflection and creative writing.

Students can further increase their knowledge and understanding of historical events by using reference sources at the library and on the Internet. Students may need assistance to learn how to use search engines and discover appropriate websites.

Titles of books for additional reading appropriate to the subject matter at this grade level are included at the end of the book.

Although many of the questions are open-ended, answer keys are included for questions with specific answers.

Share a journey through history with your students as you explore the books in the Mark Twain Media, Inc., American History series.

Discovering and Exploring the Americas
Life in the Colonies
The American Revolution
The Lewis and Clark Expedition
The Westward Movement
The California Gold Rush
The Oregon and Santa Fe Trails
Slavery in the United States
The American Civil War
Abraham Lincoln and His Times
The Reconstruction Era
Industrialization in America
The Roaring Twenties and Great Depression
World War II
America in the 1960s and 1970s

Time Line of the Roaring Twenties: 1920–1929

1913–1921   U.S. President: Woodrow Wilson

1919   The Eighteenth Amendment prohibits the sale of liquor.

1920   U.S. census = 105,710,620 people
             The Nineteenth Amendment grants women the right to vote.
             The first U.S. cross-country airmail flight is completed.
             The average life expectancy in the United States is 54.09 years.

1921–1923   U.S. President: Warren G. Harding

1921   The first skywriting takes place.

1922   *The Reader's Digest* magazine is first published.
             The first experimental car radios are developed.

1923–1929   U.S. President: Calvin Coolidge

1923   Neon signs are introduced.
             A.C. Nielson begins measuring radio audiences.
             A speech by President Harding is broadcast on the radio.
             Time magazine is first published.

1924   The first Disney cartoon, "Alice's Wonderland," is produced.
             The first "perms" for hair are available.
             The Teapot Dome Scandal becomes public.
             The Model T Ford is sold for $290.

1925   The Goodyear blimp begins sky advertising.
             The New Yorker magazine is first published.
             The "Grand Ole Opry" radio show begins in Nashville.
             Warner Brothers begins experimenting with "talkies" (movies with sound).

1926   The Book-of-the-Month Club begins.
             The first radio jingle is broadcast (Wheaties™).
             NBC is formed.
             Zippers become available.

1927   CBS is formed.
             The Holland Tunnel is opened.

1928   The first teletype machine is used.
             The first Disney cartoon with sound, "Steamboat Willie," is produced.
             The first television sets in the United States are installed in three homes.

1929   The first Academy Awards are presented.
             Experiments begin with color television.
             The stock market crashes; the Great Depression begins.

Time Line of the Great Depression: 1929–1939

1929–1933   U.S. President: Herbert Hoover
1930   U.S. census = 122,775,046 people
             "Blondie and Dagwood" becomes a daily comic strip.
             The National Unemployed Council is formed.
1931   Commercial teletype service begins.
             "The Star-Spangled Banner" becomes the national anthem.
             The Empire State Building is opened.
             The Davis-Bacon Act provides for the payment of prevailing wages to workers
                 employed on public works projects.
1932   The Lindbergh baby is kidnapped.
             The first Winter Olympics held in the United States are held at Lake Placid, NY.
             Unemployment reaches 13,000,000.
             The Norris-LaGuardia Act prohibits federal injunctions in labor disputes.
             The cost of mailing a letter rises from two cents to three cents.
1933–1945   U.S. President: Franklin D. Roosevelt
1933   Franklin D. Roosevelt begins radio "Fireside Chats."
             The first real comic book is published: *Funnies on Parade.*
             The Twenty-First Amendment repeals Prohibition.
             The National Industrial Recovery Act guarantees the rights of employees to orga-
                 nize and bargain collectively.
             Frances Perkins becomes Secretary of Labor (first woman named to a presiden-
                 tial Cabinet).
             The first drive-in movie theater opens (Camden, NJ).
             Minimum wage is set at 40 cents an hour.
1934   "High-fidelity" records become available.
             One-half of the homes in the United States have radios.
1935   IBM begins selling electric typewriters.
             The Social Security Act is signed.
1936   The BBC begins the world's first television service, three hours a day.
             The electric guitar is invented.
             LIFE, the magazine, is first published.
1937   The electrical digital calculator is invented.
             A child labor law is passed.
             Nylon is invented.
             Look magazine is first published.
             The Golden Gate Bridge opens.
1938   Disney produces its first full-length animated film, *Snow White and the Seven
                 Dwarfs.*
             The Fair Labor Standards Act establishes the 40-hour work week, the minimum
                 wage, and bans child labor in interstate commerce.
             Superman was "born."
1939   Television is demonstrated at the New York World's Fair.
             World War II begins in Europe.

Name: _____ Date: _____

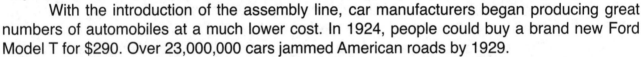

The Decade That Roared

The 1920s was one of the wildest periods in American history. When World War I ended in 1919, Americans looked to the new decade with hope for world peace. The inventions and advancements developed during the war could now be put to peaceful uses. Society rejoiced; people abandoned traditions. New rules were made—and broken.

The Eighteenth Amendment to the Constitution in 1919 made it illegal to import, sell, or manufacture alcoholic beverages—a law that was broken at every level of society.

Rapid advancements in communications, transportation, and technology caused people to coin a new phrase: "What will they think of next?"

Electricity was so new that many people were afraid of it. They bought special caps to put over electrical outlets so the electricity wouldn't spill out into the room. In 1919, only about one-third of American homes had electricity. That number had doubled by 1929.

With the introduction of the assembly line, car manufacturers began producing great numbers of automobiles at a much lower cost. In 1924, people could buy a brand new Ford Model T for $290. Over 23,000,000 cars jammed American roads by 1929.

At the beginning of the decade, movies were black and white and had no sound. Warner Brothers introduced the first color film, complete with sound, in 1929.

Passage of the Twentieth Amendment granting women the right to vote ushered in a new era of freedom for women, who began wearing new hairstyles and daring dresses so short, they showed their knees in public!

People were anxious to put thoughts of war behind them and enjoy life with a vigor never seen before. Although the decade began on a high note, it ended with fear of economic ruin. The good times came to an end with the Stock Market Crash of 1929.

1. List ten items in your home that wouldn't work without electricity.

    _____

    _____

    _____

2. Of those items, which would you miss most? Why?

    _____

    _____

    _____

    _____

Prohibition Becomes the Law

For decades many temperance groups, led mainly by women and various religious organizations, had tried to make alcohol illegal in the United States. Some blamed alcohol for the rising rate in divorces, family problems, crimes, violence, and poverty. Others felt the grain used to make alcohol could be better used for food.

By 1916, 23 of the 48 states had passed anti-saloon laws that closed taverns and prohibited the manufacture of intoxicating beverages. In 1919, the Eighteenth Amendment to the U.S. Constitution made the manufacture, sale, import, or export of liquor illegal anywhere in the United States.

The Eighteenth Amendment did not make it illegal to possess liquor or to drink it. Exceptions were also made for liquor sold for medicinal, sacramental, and industrial purposes. It also excluded fruit and grape beverages prepared for personal use at home.

Congress passed the Volstead Act to enforce Prohibition, but the government had too little money and too few people to be effective.

Even though all taverns and saloons were officially closed, illegal taverns and nightclubs—called **speakeasies**—sprang up everywhere. People smuggled liquor across the border from Canada, imported it illegally from Europe and the Caribbean Islands, and produced it in illegal factories. Prohibition gave criminals a wonderful opportunity to grow rich by providing "**bootleg**" alcohol.

1. What is your opinion of the use of alcoholic beverages? Does it cause problems?

   _____

   _____

   _____

2. Why do you think some exceptions were made to the Prohibition law?

   _____

   _____

   _____

3. Why do you think Prohibition was called "the Noble Experiment"?

   _____

   _____

4. Do you think the government has the right to ban alcohol, tobacco, drugs, or any other product? Why or why not?

   _____

   _____

   _____

Name: _____ Date: _____

Warren G. Harding's Presidency

Warren G. Harding

Born: November 2, 1865
Term of office: March 4, 1921–August 2, 1923
Occupation: Newspaper publisher
Political Party: Republican

When World War I finally ended, Warren Harding believed the country needed a "return to normalcy," and that became his campaign slogan.

Harding stressed Americanism and offered hope to people tired of war. He arranged a peace treaty signed with Germany in 1921. With Charles G. Dawes as director, the national budget was cut from six billion to three billion dollars, and at the end of 1922, there was even a surplus.

Rumors of scandal, corruption, and dishonest deals at high levels in the government began in 1922. Although Harding himself was not accused of wrong-doing, his administration is remembered for its corruption.

Charles R. Forbes, head of the Veterans Bureau and a personal friend of Harding's, was tried for bribery and conspiracy. He had authorized hundreds of millions of dollars for over-priced materials, sites, and construction.

Secretary of the Interior Albert Fall was convicted of accepting an illegal payment of $400,000 in return for turning over two valuable tracts of land to private oil companies.

Attorney General Harry Daugherty, another close friend of Harding's, stood trial twice for conspiring to defraud the government by selling government favors. Both times the juries were not able to determine a verdict, and the case was finally dropped.

1. What do you think Harding meant by a "return to normalcy"?

   _____

   _____

2. How do you think Harding felt when he learned that some of his closest friends were accused of corruption and fraud?

   _____

   _____

3. Since Harding personally appointed these men to their positions, do you think he was partly to blame for their actions? Why or why not?

   _____

   _____

   _____

Name: _____ Date: _____

Women Finally Allowed to Vote

★★★★★★★★★★★★★★★★★★★★★★★★★★★★

Nineteenth Amendment

The right of citizens of the United States to vote shall not be denied or abridged by the United States or any state on account of sex.

★★★★★★★★★★★★★★★★★★★★★★★★★★★★

The campaign for women's suffrage (the right to vote) began in the 1840s, long before the Nineteenth Amendment was finally ratified in 1920. Many states had granted women full or partial suffrage before 1920. The election of 1920 was the first time all women were allowed to vote for the president.

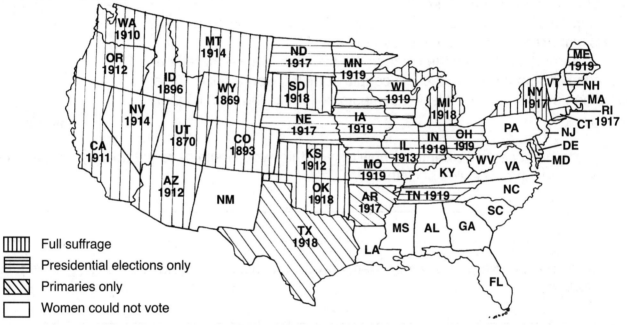

1. Which state was the first to grant full suffrage to women? _____

2. List five states that did not allow women the right to vote before the Nineteenth Amendment was passed.

_____

3. List five states that allowed women to vote in all elections before the Nineteenth Amendment was passed.

_____

4. Geographically, what stands out about states that had granted women the right to vote before the Nineteenth Amendment was passed and those that hadn't?

_____

_____

Name: _____ Date: _____

Flaming Youth

A social revolution took place among young people during the twenties. Nicknamed the "Flaming Youth," they lived for pleasure, enjoyed fast-paced music and vigorous dances, wore "scandalous" fashions and hairdos, and developed a taste for zany stunts like flagpole sitting and marathon dances.

Young women called "**flappers**" began dressing in ways that outraged their parents. Previously women's dresses had covered them completely from neck to ankles. Suddenly, fashions changed. Necklines plunged, and hemlines rose above the knees.

Young women defied authority by wearing makeup, smoking cigarettes, and cutting their hair short.

In Utah, lawmakers tried to make it illegal for women to wear "skirts higher than three inches above the ankle."

Marathons became the craze in the twenties. Dance marathons went on nonstop for days. The last couple standing won a prize. Other marathon events included kissing contests, roller-skating, and flagpole sitting.

1. If you had been a parent then, how do you think you would have felt about your daughter wearing the new styles of clothing?

   _____

   _____

2. If you had been a young person then, how do you think you would have felt about twenties' fashions?

   _____

   _____

3. What current fashion in clothing, jewelry, or hairstyle do your parents dislike?

   _____

4. How do you feel about it? _____

   _____

5. Do you think any government has the right to regulate what people wear? Why or why not?

   _____

   _____

   _____

Name: _____   Date: _____

Americans on the Go

Henry Ford built his first car in 1896. By 1908, the Ford Motor Company had produced a simple, reliable car called the Model T. Nicknamed the Tin Lizzie, its 20-horsepower engine allowed drivers to reach a top speed of 40 miles per hour.

Early Fords cost $850—a very high price for the times. At first, cars were considered "toys" only the very rich could afford. That changed when Ford introduced an efficient assembly line for production. The price of a new Ford dropped to $290 in 1924.

The Ford Motor Company described the Model T as "an inexpensive vehicle for the great multitude." People could buy cars on the install-ment plan.

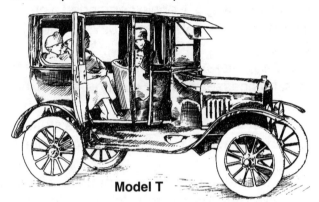

Model T

Model A

In 1927, the Ford Motor Company dis-continued making the Model T and replaced it with the more modern Model A, which sold for $395. Henry Ford announced, "a customer could have the car in any color as long as it was black."

Even at under $300 dollars, owning a car usually meant either saving for a long time or buying on credit. Most women did not have jobs outside the home. Men working at good jobs in the auto industry made between $5 and $7 per day and worked six-day weeks during the twenties. Most jobs paid much less.

1. List three ways owning a car might have affected a 1920s family that had never owned a car before.

   _____

   _____

   _____

2. Ford Motor Company was not the only important car manufacturer in the United States during the twenties. Use reference sources to find the names of three other major car makers during that time period.

   _____

   _____

3. Imagine being a child in the mid-twenties. You want to convince your parents it would be a good idea to buy an automobile. On your own paper, give three good reasons.

Name: _____   Date: _____

Automobiles Change America

Mass production of automobiles affected both society and the economy. As more people bought cars, more jobs were created in the auto industry, and wages rose. The demand for cars also created more jobs in industries that made steel, glass, rubber, petroleum, and other products used to build cars.

In a widely reported interview of the time, a farm wife was asked why her family owned a car but not a bathtub. "You can't go to town in a bathtub," she replied.

As more people drove cars, the roads became very crowded. People demanded a better road system and better roads. In 1909, the United States had only 750 miles of paved roads. By 1930, that number had risen to more than 100,000 miles.

Road construction provided jobs for crews and suppliers of materials. As more roads were built, people traveled more. Along the new roads, businesses like gas stations, diners, hot dog stands, and tourist cabins grew to meet the demand of travelers.

Car dealers and used car lots were seen for the first time. The first modern gas stations opened in 1913. By 1929, the country had 121,500—an average of more than one per mile of paved road!

Not only did automobile companies make cars, they also built millions of taxis, buses, and trucks. Between 1904 and 1929, the number of trucks registered in the United States rose from 700 to 3.4 million.

1. List three types of businesses today that wouldn't exist if people didn't have cars.

   _____

   _____

2. What businesses might have been affected when trucks and buses replaced stagecoaches and horse-drawn wagons?

   _____

   _____

3. Draw a cartoon about what the farm wife above might have said about any other aspect of owning a car in the 1920s.

Name: _____ Date: _____

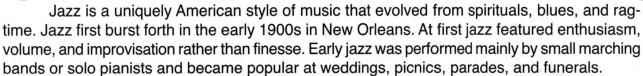

Welcome to the Jazz Age

Jazz is a uniquely American style of music that evolved from spirituals, blues, and ragtime. Jazz first burst forth in the early 1900s in New Orleans. At first jazz featured enthusiasm, volume, and improvisation rather than finesse. Early jazz was performed mainly by small marching bands or solo pianists and became popular at weddings, picnics, parades, and funerals.

Although jazz developed among Black musicians, no sound recordings remain of the earliest jazz groups. The first jazz recording in 1917 was by an all-White group who called themselves the Original Dixieland Jazz Band. Eventually New Orleans style jazz as played by Whites came to be called Dixieland Jazz.

Jazz in the 1920s involved great experimentation and discovery. For the first time, bands began featuring soloists on trumpet, saxophone, and piano. Mamie Smith had a sudden hit in 1920 with her recording of "Crazy Blues." One of the greatest jazz singers of the twenties was Bessie Smith.

Many New Orleans jazz musicians, including Louis Armstrong and Jelly Roll Morton, became famous by performing in Chicago nightclubs. Eventually a Chicago style of jazz evolved, derived from the New Orleans style, but with more emphasis on soloists and often featuring saxophones, pianos, and vocalists. Chicago jazz had tenser rhythms and more complicated textures.

Throughout the 1920s and into the 1930s, jazz continued to be a very popular form of music.

Listen to recordings made prior to 1940 of several jazz performers or groups. Samples can be found on the Internet and at your local library.

1. Which groups did you listen to? _____

   _____

2. Which was your favorite group? Why? _____

   _____

3. If your favorite group featured a soloist, what was his/her name? _____

4. Which song did you like best? _____

5. How do you feel when you listen to jazz? _____

   _____

6. What is your opinion of jazz? _____

   _____

Name: _____ Date: _____

Louis Armstrong: Master of Improvisation

Raised in poverty, Louis Armstrong became famous worldwide as a jazz trumpet player and singer. By the 1950s, Louis Armstrong had performed all over the world and was the most famous jazz musician of the time.

Born about 1901 in New Orleans, Louis Armstrong spent his first 12 years in a very poor home. His father had deserted the family. They seldom had enough to eat or decent clothing, and Louis dropped out of school after fifth grade.

When he was about 13, Louis was sent to the Colored Waifs' Home where he joined a boys' brass band. With Louis' natural ability for music as a cornet player, he soon became the star of the group. After he left the home, he played in rough clubs and dance halls in the urban slum districts of New Orleans. He couldn't afford his own cornet and had to borrow one to perform.

Louis became friends with King Oliver, a famous Black musician. After becoming part of Kid Orvy's band, his reputation grew. In 1922, Louis joined Oliver's Creole Jazz Band in Chicago.

Two years later, he joined a band in New York where he dazzled both musicians and audiences with his unique loose, springy swing style and his ability to improvise.

Previously, most jazz was played by ensembles. Rarely was any one person featured for other than a short solo. Back in Chicago in 1925, Louis led his own band and began making records playing New Orleans style jazz. The popularity of his short solos soon convinced record companies that he should be featured with other players merely providing backup.

At first, his records featured Louis playing the trumpet. Then he began singing in a rough voice that attracted listeners. His hit songs included "Savoy Blues," "Hotter Than That," "West End Blues," "Blueberry Hill," "Mack the Knife," "Hello, Dolly," and "What a Wonderful World."

1. Use a dictionary. What does *improvise* mean? _____
_____

2. Use a dictionary. What does *ensemble* mean? _____
_____

Use reference sources to find the answers.

3. One of Louis Armstrong's songs hit number one on the charts in 1964. What was the name of the song?
_____

4. What was Louis Armstrong's nickname? _____

Name: _____ Date: _____

Meet John Calvin Coolidge

As governor of Massachusetts, Calvin Coolidge attracted national attention when he called out the National Guard in response to a strike of the Boston police.

"There is no right to strike against the public safety by anybody, anywhere, anytime," he said.

1. Do you agree or disagree? Why?

_____

_____

_____

_____

Coolidge was elected vice president under President Harding in 1920. When the president died on August 3, 1929, Coolidge became president. His first challenge was to clean up the corruption that had occurred while Harding was president.

John Calvin Coolidge decided not to run for another term as president in 1928. When asked why, he replied, "Because there's no chance for advancement."

Farmers in the western part of the country did not enjoy the prosperity of the twenties. They wanted government aid, but Coolidge refused. Congress approved the McNary-Haugen Farm Relief Bill, which proposed that the government buy surplus crops and sell them abroad to raise domestic agricultural prices. Coolidge vetoed the bill in 1927 and again in 1928 because he felt the government had no business fixing prices.

Throughout his term as president, Coolidge retained very conservative policies. He opposed government intervention in private business.

2. Coolidge believed that the government should not interfere with private business. Do you agree or disagree? Why?

_____

_____

_____

Use reference sources to answer these questions about President Coolidge.

3. When and where was he born? _____

4. What was his nickname? _____

5. What political party did he belong to? _____

6. What was his occupation before going into politics? _____

7. What was his campaign slogan in the 1924 presidential election? _____

_____

Name: _____ Date: _____

At the Movies

Charlie Chaplin

If you had gone to a movie in 1925, it would probably have cost a dime. The movie would have been short, black and white, and silent. In some theaters, piano players provided background music to match the action on the screen.

The motion-picture industry flourished in the twenties as advances were made in filmmaking. Writers, directors, actors, and actresses moved to sunny southern California to make movies.

Mary Pickford and Charlie Chaplin, two of the most popular movie stars of the twenties, received huge salaries—over $500,000 a year. Other favorites included Rudolph Valentino, John Gilbert, Douglas Fairbanks, Pola Negri, Gloria Swanson, and Greta Garbo.

What types of movies did people enjoy in the twenties and thirties? Stars like Broncho Billy, Tom Mix, and William S. Hart made Westerns very popular. People enjoyed movies about crimes, like *The Great Train Robbery.* Comedies featured Charlie Chaplin, "Fatty" Arbuckle, and the Keystone Cops. Actresses like Theda Bara made love stories popular. Sentimental stories about children and/or animals were always a hit.

Although the stars have changed and movies are now in color with sound and plenty of special effects, current movies fit into many of the same categories that were popular in the twenties and thirties.

1. Making movies provided jobs for many types of people besides directors, writers, actors, and actresses. What other types of jobs are needed to make movies?

   _____

   _____

   _____

2. List a title of a modern movie for each theme.

   A Western _____

   A crime story _____

   A comedy _____

   A love story _____

   A sentimental story _____

3. What other types of movies are popular today? _____

   _____

14

Name: _____ Date: _____

Roaring Twenties Trivia

- In 1920, less than 15 percent of the people in the United States had a telephone.

- The National Negro Baseball League was organized on February 13, 1920.

- WEW in St. Louis, Missouri, aired the first weather news heard on radio in 1921.

- Henry Berliner made the first helicopter flight on June 16, 1922, at College Park, Maryland.

- The Lincoln Memorial was dedicated in Washington, D.C., on May 30, 1922.

- Henry Sullivan became the first American to swim across the English Channel on August 5, 1923.

- Yankee Stadium opened on April 18, 1923, in the Bronx as the hometown team, the New York Yankees, hosted the Boston Red Sox. A record crowd of 74,000 fans saw the action at the first three-level stadium in the country.

- Simon and Schuster, Inc., published the first "Crossword Puzzle Book" in April 1924.

- The presidential inauguration was broadcast on radio for the very first time when Calvin Coolidge took the oath of office in Washington, D.C., in March 1925.

- Gertrude Ederle, age 19, became the first American woman to swim the English Channel on August 26, 1926. She did it in a record-breaking time of 14 hours and 31 minutes.

- The Flatheads Gang committed the first armored car robbery near Pittsburgh, Pennsylvania, stealing $104,250 on March 11, 1927.

- Morris S. Frank received Buddy, the first seeing-eye dog, on April 25, 1928.

Use reference sources. Write two other interesting bits of Roaring Twenties trivia.

1. _____

    _____

    _____

2. _____

    _____

    _____

Name: _____ Date: _____

What Could You Buy for a Dollar?

During the twenties, a dollar went a long way. However, most kids only received about ten cents a week for allowance, so it took a long time to save a dollar.

1. You have one dollar to spend. If you bought a set of building blocks and went to a movie, how many pieces of penny candy could you also buy? _____

2. If you bought a board game and five candy bars, would you have enough change left from a dollar to go to a movie? _____

3. How many ice cream cones could you buy with a dollar? _____

4. How many weeks would you have to save your allowance (10 cents a week) to buy a sled? _____

5. You and three friends take the streetcar to the movie. You each have an ice cream bar as you walk home. How much did you and your friends spend in all? _____

16

Name: _____ Date: _____

Learning a New Language: Jive Talk

Many slang words and phrases came into common use in the 1920s.

If you thought someone was handing you a line of nonsense, you might tell them to stop the banana oil.

You could compliment a woman by telling her she was the eel's ankles, the bee's knees, or the cat's meow.

A stylish young man might be called a sheik. But beware if someone says you're a flat tire, because they think you're a boring person.

Match these twenties terms with their definitions. Feel free to use a dictionary, the Internet, or other resources to find the answers.

_____ 1. speakeasy	A. woman's short haircut
_____ 2. bootleg	B. an illegal tavern or nightclub
_____ 3. guff	C. dressed up; looking good
_____ 4. half-pint	D. posh; elegant
_____ 5. hep	E. being lazy
_____ 6. flapper	F. a child
_____ 7. bob	G. tease
_____ 8. razz	H. back talk
_____ 9. smackeroo	I. wool pajamas with feet
_____ 10. spiffy	J. just great
_____ 11. two bits	K. feet
_____ 12. horsefeathers	L. with it; up-to-date
_____ 13. lollygagging	M. illegal
_____ 14. mob	N. a dollar
_____ 15. ritzy	O. a quarter
_____ 16. dogs	P. gangsters
_____ 17. Dr. Dentons	Q. nonsense
_____ 18. the berries	R. stylish young woman

Name: _____ Date: _____

Twenties Scavenger Hunt

To complete this scavenger hunt, use the Internet and other reference sources to find the answers.

J.E. Clair, owner of the Acme Packing Company, bought a pro football franchise on August 27, 1921. He named the team in honor of the workers at his meat processing plant.

1. What did he name the team? _____

The National Football League franchise in Decatur, Illinois, was transferred to another city in Illinois in January 1922.

2. What team did they become? _____

In April 1923, the Firestone Tire and Rubber Company of Akron, Ohio, began the first regular production of a new product.

3. What was the product? _____

Rin Tin Tin became a famous movie star in 1923.

4. What was Rin Tin Tin? _____

The first Black American basketball team was organized in 1927.

5. What was the name of the team? _____

The first Miss America pageant was held in 1921.

6. Who was the winner? _____

The first woman to become a state governor took office in Wyoming on January 5, 1925.

7. What was her name? _____

Charles Lindbergh took off from Roosevelt Field in New York on May 20, 1927, in a small airplane. He flew nonstop to Paris, France.

8. What was the name of his plane? _____

_____

9. How long did the flight last? _____

Penicillin was discovered in 1928.

10. Who discovered it? _____

Name: _____ Date: _____

Up, Up, and Away

In 1903, the Wright brothers successfully flew an airplane for the first time. They didn't fly very far, very high, or for very long—but they did fly.

Early planes were not too reliable and were considered more of a curiosity than a future means of transportation. During World War I, however, development of airplanes progressed dramatically as military leaders realized their value both for surveillance and as weapons.

By the mid twenties, planes had become more dependable and capable of longer flights. People began to realize their potential as a new form of transportation for both people and cargo.

In 1927, Charles Lindbergh set a cross-country record when he flew from San Diego, California, to New York in 21 hours and 20 minutes. (He stopped overnight at St. Louis, Missouri.) Ten days later, Lindbergh made his most famous flight when he became the first pilot to fly solo across the Atlantic Ocean from New York to Paris, France.

Circle "F" for Fact or "O" for Opinion.

1. F O   The Wright brothers were really smart.

2. F O   The first successful airplane flight took place in 1903.

3. F O   During World War I, better and more dependable airplanes were developed.

4. F O   Early pilots must have been very brave.

5. F O   Charles Lindbergh made the first solo trans-Atlantic crossing in an airplane.

6. F O   Charles Lindbergh was a hero.

7. F O   Airplanes today are much larger and faster than they were in the twenties.

8. F O   Everyone enjoys flying.

Name: _____ Date: _____

Who's Who?

Many Americans became famous in the twenties and thirties. Use reference sources if you need help matching these people with their areas of fame.

Actress/Actor	Anthropologist	Artist	Author	Baseball player
Boxer	Composer	Dancer	Film maker	Football player
Golfer	Magician	Musician	Olympic medal winner	
Pilot	Singer	Tennis player		

1. _____ Marian Anderson

2. _____ Jelly Roll Morton

3. _____ Fred Astaire

4. _____ Pearl S. Buck

5. _____ Charlie Chaplin

6. _____ Douglas Corrigan

7. _____ Jack Dempsey

8. _____ Walt Disney

9. _____ Amelia Earhart

10. _____ George Gershwin

11. _____ Benny Goodman

12. _____ Red Grange

13. _____ Jean Harlow

14. _____ Harry Houdini

15. _____ Bobby Jones

16. _____ Joe Louis

17. _____ Margaret Mead

18. _____ Duke Ellington

19. _____ Jesse Owens

20. _____ Babe Ruth

21. _____ Bessie Smith

22. _____ John Steinbeck

23. _____ Big Bill Tilden

24. _____ Gene Tunney

25. _____ Johnny Weissmuller

Bessie Smith

Johnny Weissmuller

1920s Fiction Bestsellers

Read a review or summary of any of the novels listed. Based on the review, write a paragraph on another sheet of paper about why you would or would not be interested in reading that book.

1921
1. *Main Street*, Sinclair Lewis
2. *The Brimming Cup*, Dorothy Canfield
3. *The Mysterious Rider*, Zane Grey
4. *The Age of Innocence*, Edith Wharton
5. *The Valley of Silent Men*, James Oliver Curwood

1922
1. *If Winter Comes*, A.S.M. Hutchinson
2. *The Sheik*, Edith M. Hull
3. *Gentle Julia*, Booth Tarkington
4. *The Head of the House of Coombe*, Frances H. Burnett
5. *Simon Called Peter*, Robert Keable

1923
1. *Black Oxen*, Gertrude Atherton
2. *His Children's Children*, Arthur Train
3. *The Enchanted April*, "Elizabeth"
4. *Babbitt*, Sinclair Lewis
5. *The Dim Lantern*, Temple Bailey

1924
1. *So Big*, Edna Ferber
2. *The Plastic Age*, Percy Marks
3. *The Little French Girl*, Anne Douglas Sedgwick
4. *The Heirs Apparent*, Philip Gibbs
5. *A Gentleman of Courage*, James Oliver Curwood

1925
1. *Soundings*, A. Hamilton Gibbs
2. *The Constant Nymph*, Margaret Kennedy
3. *The Keeper of the Bees*, Gene Stratton Porter
4. *Glorious Apollo*, E. Barrington
5. *The Green Hat*, Michael Arlen

1926
1. *The Private Life of Helen of Troy*, John Erskine
2. *Gentlemen Prefer Blondes*, Anita Loos
3. *Sorrell and Son*, Warwick Deeping
4. *The Hounds of Spring*, Sylvia Thompson
5. *Beau Sabreur*, P. C. Wren

1927
1. *Elmer Gantry*, Sinclair Lewis
2. *The Plutocrat*, Booth Tarkington
3. *Doomsday*, Warwick Deeping
4. *Sorrell and Son*, Warwick Deeping
5. *Jalna*, Mazo de la Roche

1928
1. *The Bridge of San Luis Rey*, Thornton Wilder
2. *Wintersmoon*, Hugh Walpole
3. *Swan Song*, John Galsworthy
4. *The Greene Murder Case*, S. S. Van Dine
5. *Bad Girl*, V. Delmar

1929
1. *All Quiet on the Western Front*, Erich Maria Remarque
2. *Dodsworth*, Sinclair Lewis
3. *Dark Hester*, Anne Douglas Sedgwick
4. *The Bishop Murder Case*, S. S. Van Dine
5. *Roper's Row*, Warwick Deeping

Name: _____ Date: _____

The Other Side of the Coin

Not everyone in the twenties had a decade of good times. When people today read about Prohibition, gangsters, speakeasies, bootleg liquor, flappers, jive talk, dance marathons, and jazz, it's easy to get the impression gangsters hung around every street corner and all Americans partied every night.

Although the decade was marked by fun and extravaganza, not everyone lived that way. In fact, the majority of people, especially middle- and lower-class families, probably lived much the way you do now. Children went to school. They did chores around the house. They spent time with friends and family.

For some groups like Blacks, farmers, and newly-arrived immigrants, the twenties didn't roar at all. Economic conditions had changed little for Blacks in the south since the time of slavery. Prejudice was still strong. Schools and public buildings remained segregated.

Farmers in the twenties did what farmers have done for thousands of years. They plowed their fields, planted their crops, and prayed for good weather and a good harvest.

Immigrants also met prejudice as they tried to learn a new language, find jobs, and become part of a new country.

Fill in the chart to show similarities and differences between children in the 1920s and children today.

	1920s only	Now only	Then & Now
Attend school			
Watch movies			
Play video games			
Play baseball			
Help around the house			
Play board games like checkers			
Watch TV			
Listen to the radio			
Play with dolls			
Roller skate			
Ride skateboards			
Build snowmen			
Read books			

22

Name: _____ Date: _____

Evolution on Trial

In 1925, high school biology teacher John T. Scopes was accused of violating the Butler Act. This Tennessee law made it illegal for a teacher in any state-supported public school or college to teach any theory of evolution because it contradicted the Bible's account of man's creation.

Tennessee's Governor Austin Peay said, "The very integrity of the Bible in its statement of man's divine creation is denied by any theory that man descended or has ascended from any lower order of animals."

Opponents to the law believed it was a violation of the Constitution, which insures the separation of church and state.

The trial of John Scopes gained worldwide media attention. Members of the press referred to it as the "Monkey Trial" because many people thought that evolution meant humans had descended from monkeys.

The defense attorney, Clarence Darrow, argued that evolution was a valid scientific theory. He also attempted to convince the jury that the Butler Act was unconstitutional. However, he did not deny that Scopes had broken the law. Scopes was convicted and fined $100.

Darrow stated that this was "the first case of its kind since we stopped trying people for witchcraft."

The verdict was later reversed by the state supreme court, but the Butler Act remained on the books in Tennessee until 1967.

1. Why do you think a trial in Tennessee would gain worldwide attention?

   _____

   _____

   _____

   _____

2. Clarence Darrow's defense was that the law was wrong. If a law is wrong, do you think that makes it all right to ignore or break it?

   _____

   _____

   _____

   _____

3. What do you think Darrow meant by the quote above?

   _____

   _____

   _____

Name: _____ Date: _____

Review the Twenties

Match the definition in the right column with the corresponding term in the left column.

_____ 1. Charlie Chaplin

_____ 2. suffrage

_____ 3. ensemble

_____ 4. The Noble Experiment

_____ 5. improvise

_____ 6. Model A

_____ 7. Dixieland

_____ 8. Gertrude Ederle

_____ 9. spiffy

_____ 10. Babe Ruth

A. A group of musicians

B. Baseball player

C. A comedian who starred in movies

D. A type of automobile

E. Dressed up

F. Another term for Prohibition

G. Make up as you go along

H. Right to vote

I. Swam the English Channel

J. A style of jazz

Circle "T" for True or "F" for False.

11. T F The 1920s were nicknamed the Roaring Twenties because people played their radios so loud all of the time.

12. T F During the twenties, cars had a major influence on Americans.

13. T F Calvin Coolidge's administration was marked by scandal and corruption.

14. T F Charles Lindbergh made the first solo flight across the Atlantic Ocean.

15. T F Women who cut their hair short and wore short skirts and makeup were called flappers.

16. T F Although jazz began in the twenties, it didn't become popular until the sixties.

17. T F Warren G. Harding died while president.

18. T F Jazz combined rock and roll, opera, and classical music into a new form.

19. T F Louis Armstrong grew up in a rich home in New York City.

20. T F None of the movies made during the twenties or thirties were Westerns.

Name: _____ Date: _____

The Millionaire Miner

When Hoover graduated with a mining engineering degree in 1895, he had $40 in his pocket and no job prospects. He ended up working for $2.50 a day as a pick-and-shovel miner in a California gold mine. His experience, hard work, talents, and ambition did not lack a challenge for long, though.

At age 23, he managed a successful gold mine in Western Australia. From there he went to China as a mining consultant. He spent time with other mining operations in Europe, Russia, Southwest Asia, and Africa.

By 1908, Hoover owned a worldwide business with offices in France, England, and the United States and was a millionaire several times over.

Although he probably could have made another fortune during World War I when the demand for ore and metal increased greatly, Hoover agreed to head the Commission for Relief in Belgium. He worked without pay to organize a successful relief program to feed ten million starving people in Belgium. Then he accepted the position of Food Administrator in the United States and later, Chief of the Supreme Allied Economic Council.

Before becoming president, Hoover led a colorful life. Orphaned at the age of eight, he was raised by his uncle in Oregon. While at Stanford University, Hoover founded his own fraternity: the Barbarians.

Hoover's success led to his appointment as Secretary of Commerce under Presidents Harding and Coolidge. When Coolidge chose not to seek reelection in 1928, the Republicans nominated Hoover.

1. From what you read, what impresses you the most about Herbert Hoover? Explain your answer.

   _____

   _____

   _____

   _____

2. Why do you think a successful businessman like Hoover would agree to take on the responsibility for feeding ten million people and agree to do it without pay?

   _____

   _____

   _____

   _____

Name: _____ Date: _____

The Crash Heard Around the World

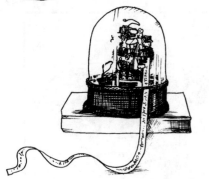

Market in Panic

Stocks Are Dumped

Throughout the twenties, people spent money much more freely than ever before. More products were available; more people had jobs, and wages were higher. People bought on credit. As stock prices steadily climbed throughout the decade, people often invested everything they had, mortgaged their homes, and even borrowed money to buy stocks. They thought the prosperity of the twenties would last forever.

In the fall of 1929, investors who had bought stocks on credit began to sell. As more stocks sold, prices fell. Investors panicked, especially those who had bought stocks on margin (bought at a lower price, promising to pay the rest later). Between Black Thursday (October 24, 1929) and Terrible Tuesday (October 29, 1929) so many shares of stock were sold that the market collapsed completely. In one day, stock values dropped $10–$15 billion.

Not all Americans had invested in the stock market, but almost everyone felt an immediate effect of the crash. Most Americans kept their savings in banks that had invested the funds in the stock market. When the stock market crashed, the banks couldn't return the money to investors. In one terrible week, rich, middle-class, and poor people lost everything.

Over 1,300 banks went broke in 1930. Another 2,300 failed the following year. The stock market crash brought the good times of the twenties to a screeching halt. Although no one yet realized the extent of the problem, the stock market crash began the Great Depression, which lasted until the mid 1940s.

Unemployment went from three percent in 1925 to 25 percent in 1932. Many people who still had jobs were required to take cuts in pay to keep their jobs.

1. How do you think people felt if they had all their savings in a bank that suddenly went broke?

    _____

    _____

    _____

2. Use a dictionary. What is the economic meaning of *depression*?

    _____

    _____

3. On your own paper, create an illustration that summarizes this paragraph:

    As more people lost their jobs, they had less money to spend. Less people spending money meant stores sold fewer products and needed fewer workers. Since fewer products were purchased, factories produced less, and more people lost their jobs.

Name: _____   Date: _____

The 1930s

    The 1920s may have begun with a bang, but the 1930s opened with a crash. The effects of the October 1929 Stock Market Crash echoed across the nation as the new decade began. Investors lost tens of billions of dollars. Over a million people lost their life savings in the stock market crash. Even those who had no money in stocks felt the chain reaction that resulted.

    People in the thirties faced many new challenges as businesses and industries shut down and banks collapsed. Millions of people found themselves unemployed and homeless. Schools closed in rural areas. An estimated 2.2 million children were not attending school in 1933. Between 1930 and 1935, as many as 750,000 farms were lost because of bankruptcy.

    President Herbert Hoover underestimated the severity of the problem as he assured people that the crisis was "a passing incident in our national lives." Hoover did not believe the federal government should provide relief or jobs to individuals. He thought private charities, together with city and state governments, were responsible for helping those in need.

    During the thirties, many people relied on soup kitchens for food. They stood in bread lines to buy day-old bread. They looked to the government to solve the massive unemployment problem. Men walked around with their pockets turned inside out to show they were broke. Millions learned to make do with what they had, because they couldn't afford new clothing, furniture, appliances, or automobiles.

    Advances in technology, communications, and transportation continued but at a much slower pace than in the previous decade.

1. Use a dictionary. What does *bankruptcy* mean? _____

   _____

2. Do you agree or disagree with Hoover that charities instead of the government were responsible for those in need? Why?

   _____

   _____

   _____

3. Why do you think advances in technology, communication, and transportation slowed in the thirties?

   _____

   _____

Name: _____   Date: _____

What's New?

Circle all the products that were introduced in the twenties and thirties, and people still use today.

1920   Pogo™ sticks

1921   Band-Aids™
Wrigley's™ gum

1922   Eskimo Pie™
The Readers Digest magazine

1923   Welch's™ grape jelly
Time magazine

1924   Wheaties™ cereal
spiral-bound notebooks
Kleenex™
crossword puzzle books
permanents for hair

1925   *The New Yorker* magazine

1926   zippers

1927   Hostess™ cakes

1928   Rice Krispies™

1930   *Nancy Drew* mysteries

1931   Scotch™ Tape
electric razors
Scrabble™
Alka-Seltzer™

1933   Mickey Mouse™ watches
comic books

1934   hi-fi records

1935   parking meters
paperback books
electric typewriters
MONOPOLY™ game
first sold by Parker Brothers

1936   electric guitars
LIFE magazine

1937   nylon
Look magazine
Wheat Chex™

1938   *Jack and Jill* magazine

1939   air-conditioned cars

1.   Which of these products surprised you the most that they had been available so long ago? Why?

_____

_____

_____

Name: _____ Date: _____

Herbert Hoover, President

Born: August 10, 1874
Term as President: March 4, 1929, to March 4, 1933
Political Party: Republican

President Herbert Hoover

During Hoover's presidential campaign, the country was flourishing. Most people expected the economic prosperity to continue indefinitely. In a spirit of optimism, Hoover promised "… a chicken in every pot and a car in every garage."

1. What do you think Hoover really meant by that?

    _____

    _____

    _____

    _____

    Although the economic prosperity of the twenties continued in most industries until the stock market crash, farmers were already having problems. As they increased efficiency and put more land into farming, prices dropped. Trying to produce more crops made prices drop even lower.

    In response, Congress passed the Agricultural Marketing Act of 1929, which established the first large-scale aid to farmers during peacetime.

    Although Hoover began his term as president on an optimistic note, that ended less than eight months later when the stock market crashed in October 1929, plunging the United States into what became known as the Great Depression.

    After the Depression began, farm prices continued to drop. By 1932, government funds ran out, and prices plunged to a new low.

    Hoover went from being a very popular president to one of the most disliked men in America. By the 1932 presidential election, the entire country had been affected. Hoover did not have a chance for reelection.

2. Do you think the Great Depression was Hoover's fault? Why or why not?

    _____

    _____

    _____

3. Would you have voted for Hoover in 1932? Why or why not?

    _____

    _____

    _____

Name: _____ Date: _____

Meet Young Franklin D. Roosevelt

Franklin Delano Roosevelt

Born: January 30, 1882, in Hyde Park, New York
Profession: Lawyer
Term as President: March 4, 1933, to April 12, 1945
Political Party: Democratic

Franklin D. Roosevelt grew up in a wealthy New York family. He spent summers vacationing in Europe and never attended school until he was 14 years old. His family provided private tutors, and his mother supervised his education.

As a young man, Roosevelt enjoyed bird watching and natural history. He enjoyed sports, particularly swimming and hiking. Reading adventure stories and stamp collecting were two of his other favorite pastimes.

In 1896, Roosevelt attended Groton School, a private preparatory school in Massachusetts. He went on to Harvard and then to Columbia Law School in 1904. Against his mother's advice, he married Eleanor Roosevelt, a distant cousin.

Roosevelt's early political career included two terms in the New York state senate (1910–1913) and an appointment as assistant secretary of the Navy (1913–1920). He resigned to campaign for the vice presidency in 1920 but lost the election.

As a result of polio in 1921, Roosevelt lost the use of his legs. He was unable to walk without crutches. His mother wanted him to retire from politics, but Roosevelt had other ideas.

With the help of his wife, Roosevelt remained active behind the scenes until he ran for governor of New York in 1928. Most people were unaware of the extent of his disability when he was governor and later president.

1. Use reference sources. Who was the Democratic candidate who ran for president with Roosevelt in 1920?

   _____

2. Since his family was wealthy, Roosevelt could have retired and spent the rest of his life as an invalid with servants and nurses to care for him. Instead, he chose an active, productive career. What does that tell you about his character?

   _____

   _____

   _____

   _____

Name: _____ Date: _____

New President, New Deal

     In 1928, the Republican candidate, Herbert Hoover, received the electoral votes from all but seven states. After the Great Depression began, the tide turned. Many people blamed Hoover and the Republicans for the economic problems of the country.

     In the 1932 presidential election, only six states remained Republican. Franklin D. Roosevelt, the Democratic candidate, received the electoral votes from 42 states.

1. Draw two pie charts or two of another type of graph to show a comparison between the results of the 1928 and 1932 presidential elections.

     To help the country and its people recover, Roosevelt and Congress quickly passed several measures to relieve poverty, reduce unemployment, speed economic recovery, and stabilize the banking industry. Roosevelt's "New Deal" programs didn't provide an immediate cure, but they did ease hard times by addressing basic needs and giving new hope to Americans by setting the groundwork for a gradual recovery.

     Although the Great Depression hadn't ended by the time of the 1936 election, voters stayed with Roosevelt and the Democrats. He received the electoral votes from every state except Maine and Vermont.

     When George Washington refused to run for a third term as president, he set a precedent that all other presidents followed—until Franklin D. Roosevelt. Not only did Roosevelt run for a third term and win, he was also elected for a fourth term.

2. Why do you think the term "New Deal" was used for Roosevelt's programs?

_____

_____

_____

3. Do you think there should be a limit to how long a person can hold a political office? Why or why not?

_____

_____

_____

Name: _____ Date: _____

President Roosevelt

President Franklin D. Roosevelt

When Franklin D. Roosevelt took office on March 4, 1933, more than 13,000,000 people were out of work, banks had failed, and the country was in trouble.

Roosevelt immediately called a special session of Congress and pushed for needed legislation to deal with the banking crisis, economic issues, and changes to the liquor law.

Roosevelt's domestic New Deal programs introduced reforms that involved the government directly in national and economic affairs. During the first hundred days of his administration, he passed many new programs including the Economy Act, which reduced government salaries and pensions. A new law made low alcohol beer legal, even though Prohibition was still in effect.

No session of Congress had ever produced so much important legislation. Roosevelt's success was partly due to widespread desperation and partly to his ability as a strong leader.

Roosevelt and his advisors felt it was important that people see him as a strong leader. To minimize his disability, he was seated first at dinners, and his wheelchair was removed before other guests arrived. The press cooperated by not reporting the extent of his physical problems and publishing pictures that showed him standing (which he could do for short periods of time or with the help of a couple of strong men) or seated only in regular chairs. Many people were unaware that he couldn't walk.

Previous presidents had relied heavily on advice from other politicians who belonged to the same political party. Understanding the enormity of the problems facing the nation, Roosevelt turned for advice to a group called the Brain Trust—faculty members from Columbia University and Harvard.

1. Do you think the press would conceal a disability for a president or major leader today? Why or why not?

   _____

   _____

2. Why do you think Roosevelt didn't want people to know the extent of his disability?

   _____

   _____

   _____

3. Do you think the Brain Trust was a good idea? Why or why not?

   _____

   _____

Name: _____ Date: _____

Conduct an Interview

You are a reporter for a newspaper in December 1929. Your boss sent you to write an article about the effects of the stock market crash on one formerly wealthy family who lost everything.

Write 12 questions you could ask a person from such a family during an interview to prepare an article for your paper.

1. _____
   _____

2. _____
   _____

3. _____
   _____

4. _____
   _____

5. _____
   _____

6. _____
   _____

7. _____
   _____

8. _____
   _____

9. _____
   _____

10. _____
    _____

11. _____
    _____

12. _____
    _____

Name: _____ Date: _____

The Lame Duck Amendment

The purpose of the Twentieth Amendment, ratified in 1933, was to shorten the time between the election and the date when government officials took office.

Under the original Constitution, a new president and vice president took office on March 4 following the November election. If the incumbent president and vice president had not been reelected or had decided not to run, they remained in office for four months after the election. The Twentieth Amendment moved that date up to January 20.

Newly elected members of Congress had to wait to take office until the next regular session of Congress began in December of the year following the election—a full 13 months! In the meantime, those who had not run for office or won reelection retained their positions for over a year. With the change, new members of Congress begin their terms on January 3 following the election.

Section 3 states that if the president-elect dies before taking office, the vice president-elect shall become the president.

The amendment also states that if no president has been selected by January 20, the newly elected vice president shall become acting president until a president is chosen.

If neither the president nor vice president has been chosen by January 20, Congress will decide who becomes acting president.

1. Why do you think people wanted to change the dates when the president, vice president, and legislators took office?

   _____

   _____

   _____

2. Why do you think this was called the "Lame Duck" Amendment?

   _____

   _____

   _____

3. Do you think it was fair to allow the newly elected vice president to become president if the president-elect died before taking office? Why or why not?

   _____

   _____

   _____

4. Why is it important to be very specific about who becomes president?

   _____

   _____

Name: _____ Date: _____

Math Facts

1. In 1933, the minimum wage was set at 40 cents an hour. How much _____ would a person earn each week working 10 hours a day, six days a week?

2. What would that person's annual income be? _____

3. The first parking meter was installed in Oklahoma City, Oklahoma, in _____ 1935. How many years ago was that?

4. There were 750 miles of paved roads in the United States in 1909. By _____ 1930, that number had gone up to 100,000 miles. On an average, how many miles of road would have had to have been built per year during that 21-year time period? Round your answer to the nearest mile.

5. The world-famous Mickey Mouse™ watch first became available in _____ 1933. It sold for $2.75. At 40 cents an hour, how long would a person have to work to pay for a Mickey Mouse™ watch? Round your answer to the nearest hour.

6. In 1937, wages for workers at U.S. Steel were raised to $5 a day. How _____ much did they earn per hour if they worked ten-hour days?

7. The U.S. Treasury Department announced in October 1925 that they _____ had fined 29,620 people for (alcohol) Prohibition violations. The fines totaled $5,000,000. What was the average amount of fine per person? Round your answer to the nearest dollar.

8. Herbert Hoover's first job after college was as a pick-and-shovel miner _____ for $2.50 a day. How much did he earn for a six-day workweek?

9. The first MONOPOLY™ games sold for $4 each. Working with a friend, _____ Charles Darrow could make six games a day. How much would they have taken in if they had sold all the games they made in 15 days?

10. In 1924, a Ford Model T sold for $290. The Model A introduced in 1927 _____ sold for $395. What was the percent of increase in the cost? Round your answer to the nearest percent.

11. In 1920, less than 15 percent of the people in the United States had a _____ telephone. The population of the United States in 1920 was 105,710,620. What would be 15 percent of that number?

12. By 1930, the population of the United States had risen to 122,775,046. _____ How many more people were there than in 1920?

Name: _____ Date: _____

The Repeal of Prohibition

The Eighteenth Amendment prohibiting alcohol was ratified by voters in three-quarters of the states, yet no law was ever so violently opposed and ignored at all levels of American society. As a result, many people felt Prohibition promoted disrespect for the law.

1. Do you agree or disagree? Why?

    _____

    _____

    _____

Almost as soon as Prohibition was passed, people began working to repeal it. They felt that the law was an invasion of the private lives of citizens.

2. Do you agree or disagree? Why?

    _____

    _____

    _____

Another argument for repeal was that Prohibition generated organized crime and that the profits that could be made from illegal alcohol promoted corruption at almost every level of government.

3. Do you agree or disagree? Why?

    _____

    _____

    _____

In 1933, Section 1 of the Twenty-First Amendment to the Constitution ended Prohibition. According to Section 2, if any state, territory, or possession of the United States wanted to make alcohol illegal, they had the right to do so. It would then be illegal to import or manu-facture alcohol in those areas.

4. Write three reasons of your own why alcohol should or should not be illegal.

    _____

    _____

    _____

    _____

    _____

Name: _____ Date: _____

Isolationism

During much of its history, the United States has maintained an **isolationist** policy, believing the country's best interest would be served by avoiding alliances with other nations.

This policy of isolationism kept the United States out of World War I until 1917. When the United States finally declared war, leaders felt our country was obligated to "make the world safe for democracy."

After World War I, President Woodrow Wilson presented a plan for a general association of nations that became the League of Nations in 1920. Although Wilson was a member of the committee that drafted the charter, the U.S. Senate never ratified it.

Article X of the charter stated that if any nation threatened a member country, all members of the league would be obligated to help, even if it meant war.

American diplomats encouraged the league's activities and unofficially attended meetings, but the United States never became a member of the League of Nations.

World War I was called "the war to end all wars." However, it soon became clear that all countries would not be democracies and nations would continue to fight wars. Faced with the problems of the Great Depression, the tendency towards isolationism increased. Many people decided to ignore the problems in other countries, choosing rather to focus on and solve problems at home.

During the 1930s, new dictators rose in Germany, Japan, Italy, and Russia, causing a flood of immigration to the United States. Instead of welcoming new arrivals, Congress cut the number of immigrants allowed in an effort to control and restrict foreign influences.

In the early thirties, Congress also voted to restrict foreign trade to protect the U.S. economy and to remain neutral in foreign disputes.

1. What do you think the phrase "make the world safe for democracy" means?

   _____

   _____

   _____

2. If you had been a member of the Senate, would you have voted to join the League of Nations? Why or why not?

   _____

   _____

   _____

3. Do you agree or disagree with the policy of isolationism? Why?

   _____

   _____

   _____

Name: _____ Date: _____

What Happened When?

Use the time line on page 3 to complete this activity.

1. When and where were the first Winter Olympics in the U.S. held?

    _____

2. What were two magazines first published in the 1930s?

    _____

3. What was the title of Disney's first full-length animated movie?

    _____

4. Who was the president in 1937? _____

5. When did the "The Star-Spangled Banner" become the official national anthem?

    _____

6. How many homes in the United States had radios in 1934? _____

7. Which opened first, the Golden Gate Bridge or the Empire State Building?

    _____

8. How much did it cost to mail a letter in 1932? _____

9. Who was the first woman to become a member of the president's Cabinet?

    _____

10. How many people were unemployed in 1932? _____

11. What was minimum wage in 1933? _____

12. Which amendment repealed Prohibition? _____

13. When was the Social Security Act signed? _____

14. Which were available first: electric guitars, electric typewriters, or electric calculators?

    _____

15. What was the name of the first comic book published? _____

Fun Facts About the Thirties

- In 1930, Charles Creighton and Jim Hagis made the record books when they drove from New York to Los Angeles and back. That wasn't the first time such a trip had been undertaken. But it was the first time anyone did it driving backwards all the way! They never drove faster than 14 miles an hour, and the trip took a total of 42 days.

- Ruth Wakefield, owner of the Toll House Inn in Whitman, Massachusetts, invented chocolate chip cookies by accident in 1930. Because she had run out of baking cocoa to make chocolate cookies for her guests, she substituted small pieces of a Nestle's Chocolate Bar. Instead of chocolate cookies, she invented a delicious surprise. In return for allowing them to print her recipe for Toll House Cookies on the candy wrapper, the Nestle Company offered her a lifetime supply of free chocolate.

- Reading became a popular form of entertainment during the thirties. Penguin Books, launched in England in 1935, pioneered the "paperback revolution" by publishing inexpensive classics and new novels.

- "Elm Farm Ollie" became the first cow to fly in an airplane in 1930. While in flight over St. Louis, the cow was milked. The milk was sealed in little paper containers and then parachuted over the city.

- The first U.S. federal tax on gasoline was enacted in 1932. The rate back then? A penny per gallon!

- Pinball machines were illegal in Atlanta, Georgia, in 1939.

- A U.S. Congressman introduced a resolution in 1932 requiring all Civil Service employees to "sing, write or recite the words to 'The Star-Spangled Banner'" by memory.

- The June 7, 1938, cover of *LIFE* magazine showed the latest in campus fashions of the day, which included saddle shoes.

- Walt Disney's famous duck made his first appearance on film in 1934 as a minor character in "The Wise Little Hen." Donald Duck went on to quack his way to stardom.

- In 1939, the King and Queen of England visited President and Mrs. Franklin D. Roosevelt. In honor of the grand event, the White House staff prepared gourmet foods of the United States. It was the first time the King and Queen had tasted hot dogs.

Use the Internet or other reference sources to find two other fun facts about the thirties. Write them on your own paper.

Name: _____ Date: _____

New Deal Programs

One popular New Deal program was the **Civilian Conservation Corps (CCC)**. Established by Congress in 1933, the CCC provided needy young men with jobs in forests and national parks.

The program had two main purposes: employment and training for young men and conservation of natural resources including timber, soil, and water. Unemployed, unmarried men between the ages of 17 and 23 were eligible to join the CCC. They were paid $30 a month and lived in work camps. About three million men were employed by the CCC.

Workers carved out roads and hiking trails, cleaned up beaches, and cleared camping sites to develop national parks. They laid down telephone lines and constructed fire observation towers. Reforestation projects included planting about two million trees from Texas to North Dakota.

The **Works Progress Administration (WPA)** began in 1935 when the president and Congress decided to shift federal relief funds to providing useful employment. By 1943, the program had provided jobs for nine million workers in road maintenance and construction of buildings and facilities. The **National Youth Administration (NYA)** program also provided four million part-time jobs.

Projects included the construction of schools, dormitories, hospitals, airports, docks, and ports plus slum clearance, flood control, and rural electrification. The WPA also provided jobs for artists (painting murals on public buildings), writers (conducting research projects), and actors and actresses (touring and performing in rural areas) through the Federal Writers, Theater, and Arts Program.

1. Why do you think the CCC was a very popular program? _____

    _____

2. How did the work done by members of the CCC help all Americans?

    _____

    _____

3. Do you think it is the government's obligation to provide work for people who are unemployed? Why or why not?

    _____

    _____

4. What do you think is better: providing jobs or providing welfare? Why?

    _____

    _____

Name: _____ Date: _____

Desperate Times, Desperate People, Desperate Actions

When the International Apple Shippers Association came up with an oversupply of fruit in 1930, they also came up with a unique solution. They sold apples on credit to people who were unemployed. The unemployed stood on street corners selling apples for five cents each.

This trend led to others besides apple sellers peddling everything from watches to patent medicines. Cities eventually had to pass laws banning street vendors as a public nuisance.

People who were desperate sometimes turned to pawnshops. In exchange for a ring, watch, or other treasured item, pawnshops might loan a person a few dollars to buy groceries, pay the rent, or keep the car from being repossessed.

In March 1933, about 1,000 people a day all across the country lost their homes due to foreclosures. When people couldn't pay their rent or mortgages, they were evicted from their homes.

Desperate for places to live, people moved into abandoned factories and warehouses. Shanty towns called **Hoovervilles** sprang up in empty lots, under bridges, in city dumps, and along major highways.

People scrounged through city dumps, construction sites, and trash bins for materials to build shelters. Abandoned cars and stacks of wooden fruit boxes became homes for desperate families. They lacked electricity and running water. Crime, disease, and hunger filled these shanty towns.

Those who managed to keep or find jobs often had to take a cut in pay and/or a cut in hours. People took in boarders to help pay the bills and share expenses. Women and children worked when they could. People begged when they had no other choice.

Blacks and immigrants were affected as much or more by the lack of jobs. Often the last hired and the first fired, they earned less, worked harder, and had less job security even in good times. Blacks who had been tenant farmers in the South migrated to the North hoping to find work.

1. How did the Apple Shippers Association's solution help the Association, consumers, and the unemployed?

   _____

   _____

   _____

2. Why do you think the shanty towns were nicknamed Hoovervilles or Hoover Cities?

   _____

   _____

   _____

Name: _____   Date: _____

An Alphabet Soup of New Deal Programs

Besides the CCC, the WPA, and the NYA, Roosevelt's New Deal included a whole alphabet soup of other programs. Even Roosevelt himself was often referred to as FDR.

Use reference sources to find the answers.

One of Roosevelt's earliest concerns was to stabilize banks and give depositors a sense of security. The FDIC insured the savings of depositors up to $5,000 at all Federal Reserve banks.

1. What did FDIC stand for? _____

The TVA was authorized to manage local resources and construct a series of hydroelectric dams to provide cheap power.

2. What did TVA stand for? _____

Created in 1933, FERA granted three billion dollars to states to fund work projects for unemployed adults.

3. What did FERA stand for? _____

The AAA provided crop reduction subsidies to stabilize prices and loans for overdue farm mortgages.

4. What did AAA stand for? _____

Another federal program, the HOLC, helped people in danger of losing their homes due to foreclosure by allowing them to refinance with low-interest loans.

5. What did HOLC stand for? _____

The NRA was designed to assist industry and labor by establishing voluntary codes and standards for wages, working hours, child labor, etc. As a whole, this program had many faults, but it did bring about shorter workdays and five-day workweeks.

6. What did NRA stand for? (Note: this was not the National Rifle Association.)

_____

Name: _____ Date: _____

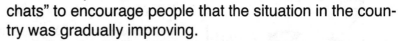

Let's Listen to the Radio

After the stock market crash of 1929, radio broadcasting was one of the few businesses that prospered during hard times. With millions out of work and money for recreation scarce, radio provided cheap entertainment. Radio also brought people from different classes and different parts of the country together in a new way. Farmers in Iowa could listen to the same music as party-goers in New York. A poor woman in Mississippi could enjoy the same radio adventures as a rich man in California.

Besides live music and records, people listened to political speeches, sports programs, and weather forecasts. Franklin D. Roosevelt kept Americans informed with a series of "fireside chats" to encourage people that the situation in the country was gradually improving.

Radio also brought situation comedies and dramas into the homes of millions of Americans. Soap operas dominated the daytime airwaves. The most popular program of the thirties was "Amos 'n' Andy," which attracted as many as 30 million listeners each week.

Other popular serials were "Fibber McGee and Molly," "Little Orphan Annie," "The Green Hornet," "The Shadow," "Jack Armstrong, All-American Boy," "Dick Tracy," and "The Lone Ranger." Many radio stars like Jack Benny went on to make names for themselves in movies and TV. In radio, a person's voice and personality were important, but how they looked didn't matter. The audience could imagine the character any way they wished, based on what they heard.

Besides providing entertainment and information, radio also broadcast advertisements. Even if people couldn't afford new products, they could listen to descriptions—and dream of the day when their lives might be better.

One illustration of the impact radio had on Americans was the October 30, 1938, broadcast of the science fiction play "War of the Worlds" about the invasion of Martians. A million listeners panicked as they mistook the play for a newscast.

1. What types of programs did people listen to in the 1930s that people today can still hear?

   _____

   _____

2. People in the thirties relied on the radio for information and entertainment. What source do people rely on today?

   _____

3. How did movies and television affect the importance of the appearance of the characters?

   _____

   _____

Name: _____ Date: _____

Meet Eleanor Roosevelt

Use reference sources to fill in the blanks.

Eleanor Roosevelt became the most active first lady to live in the White House.

1. Although she grew up in a wealthy family, Eleanor Roosevelt's childhood must have been far from happy. When she was eight years old, her _____ died, and she went to live with her _____ _____, a very stern woman.

2. Eleanor was deeply attached to her father, an alcoholic who was often away for treatments and was seldom allowed to visit her. He died when she was _____ years old.

3. Eleanor was sent to a boarding school in _____ when she was 15.

4. Long before her husband, _____, was elected president, Eleanor had been an active woman, interested in politics and social conditions. She did charity work in Albany, New York, and worked for the Red Cross during World War I.

5. Unlike most previous first ladies, Eleanor Roosevelt did not believe in staying quietly in the background. She traveled extensively visiting hospitals and schools, held weekly press conferences, and wrote articles and a newspaper column titled, "_____."

6. Eleanor seemed to enjoy adventure. At the Winter Olympics at Lake Placid, New York, she took a ride down the bobsled run. She rode over _____ Dam in a bucket. On her way to the Democratic National Convention in 1940, the pilot let her fly the plane.

7. Never one to back away from controversial issues, Eleanor took a stand when members of the Daughters of the American Revolution prevented Marian Anderson, a black singer, from performing at Constitution Hall in Washington, D.C., in 1939. Angrily, Eleanor resigned from the group and organized an alternate site for the concert at the _____ _____.

8. Eleanor remained active after her husband's death and became the U.S. delegate to the _____ from 1945 to 1953.

9. What was Eleanor Roosevelt's maiden name? _____

10. Who was her famous uncle? _____

From Rags to Riches

When Charles Darrow lost his job as a salesman of heating and engineering equipment, he tried to support his family by taking any kind of work he could get, but it wasn't enough. He spent his free time inventing toys and games. He had several interesting ideas, but no one was willing to buy them.

Remembering the "good old days" when he and his wife had visited a seaside resort in Atlantic City, New Jersey, Darrow sketched out the street names. He added railroads to carry vacationers to the resort and utilities to service the area. He divided the streets into parcels worth varying amounts.

Darrow made little houses and hotels with scraps of wooden molding discarded by a lumber yard. He painted the board and typed title cards for the properties. He used colored buttons for game pieces, dice, and lots of play money. He called the game MONOPOLY™.

Not only did Darrow and his wife enjoy MONOPOLY™, but when friends played, they also liked the game so much they wanted their own sets. Darrow made copies for them. Soon the demand increased, and he began selling the games for $4 each.

As more people played MONOPOLY™ with their friends, Darrow got more orders and began making two games a day. Encouraged, Darrow made up a few sets and offered them to a department store in Philadelphia. They sold.

Darrow and a friend increased production to six sets a day, but orders piled up faster than they could fill them. Darrow knew he would either have to borrow money to go into production on a larger scale or sell the game to another company.

He wrote to the Parker Brothers game company. They turned him down because they felt MONOPOLY™ was too complicated and took too long to play. It would never be accepted by the public, they said.

Darrow enlisted the help of a printer to produce 5,000 sets. Department stores ordered so many sets Darrow found himself working 14 hours a day. A major New York toy and game store (F.A.O. Schwartz) bought 200 sets.

When a friend called Sally Barton (daughter of George Parker) to rave about the marvelous game he had bought in New York, she told her husband, who was currently president of the company. They tried the game, and they found themselves playing it until 1 A.M.

Barton wrote to Darrow and met with him three days later. Parker Brothers offered to buy the game and pay royalties on all sets sold on condition that they could make some revisions in the rules. Darrow agreed. The royalties from sales of MONOPOLY™ allowed Darrow to retire as a millionaire at the age of 46.

Work with a small group to invent your own board game. Draw it on poster board. It could be similar to MONOPOLY™ using places in your city or based on another theme, like a sport, movie, book, or cartoon character. Gather any game pieces needed, write up the rules, and play the game.

Name: _____ Date: _____

The Thirties: Cause and Effect

A **cause** is an event that produces a result. An **effect** is the result produced. For each cause, write a possible effect.

Cause	Effect
1. Banks across the country closed after the stock market crashed.	_____ _____ _____
2. Parts of the country experienced a drought for several years.	_____ _____ _____
3. Millions of people were unemployed during the thirties.	_____ _____ _____
4. Eleanor Roosevelt was a very active first lady.	_____ _____ _____
5. Congress set up work programs like the CCC and WPA.	_____ _____ _____
6. The Lame Duck Amendment changed the date new members of Congress took office.	_____ _____ _____

Name: _____   Date: _____

Thirties Scavenger Hunt

Use the Internet and other reference sources to find the answers below.

Herbert Hoover's vice president, Charles Curtis, was a Native American.

1. To what tribe did he belong? _____

In 1930, this baseball great signed a two-year contract with the New York Yankees for the huge sum of $80,000.

2. Who was he? _____

An actor who later became a national political figure made his movie debut in 1937 when he was 26 years old in the Warner Brothers movie *Love is in the Air.*

3. What was his name? _____

In May 1932, Public Enemy Number One, Al Capone, was sent to the Atlanta Penitentiary.

4. What was he convicted of? _____

The first episode of "The Lone Ranger" was heard on radio in 1933 and ran until 1954. Several different radio actors played the part of the Lone Ranger, including Clayton Moore from 1949 to 1952. The part of his faithful companion, Tonto, was played for almost the entire time by John Todd, a bald Irishman. On radio and later on television and in films, every episode of "The Lone Ranger" began with the same music.

5. What was the name of the song?

_____

6. Who played Tonto after it became a TV show?

_____

Before the "Singing Cowboy" became famous in movies in the thirties, he worked as a telegraph operator. He made more than 90 Westerns during his career and had a TV show that ran for six seasons.

7. Who was the "Singing Cowboy"? _____

Fred Waring invented the Waring Blender. However, he was more famous for his other occupation.

8. What was Fred Waring's occupation? _____

Band leader and clarinetist Artie Shaw became famous in the thirties.

9. What was Artie Shaw's real name? _____

Name: _____ Date: _____

The Social Security Act of 1935

Another important law passed while Franklin Roosevelt was president was the Social Security Act of 1935. This act set up six specific programs and established methods of taxes to fund them.

Old-Age Benefits (later called Social Security) was funded by federal taxes deducted from workers. When workers retired at age 65, they became eligible to receive a monthly check. Benefits were extended to widows and dependent children of retired workers.

States taxed employers to fund the **Unemployment Compensation** program to provide income when people were out of work.

The other four programs were forms of welfare funded by grants from the federal government and administered by the states. They included **Old-Age Assistance**, **Aid to Dependent Children**, **Maternal and Child Welfare**, and **Aid to the Blind**.

Old-Age Assistance and Aid to the Blind programs were designed to supplement Old-Age Benefits or to provide benefits for those not eligible for Old-Age Benefits.

Maternal and Child Welfare provided health care to poor mothers and their children and was designed to protect and care for homeless, neglected, or disabled children.

Aid to Dependent Children helped support children living with only one parent or with relatives other than parents.

The first Social Security cards were issued in 1937 when the government began collecting Social Security taxes. Each person received a unique number used to keep track of earnings and taxes paid. Money was placed into a trust fund to be used to pay benefits, cover the costs of administering the program, and earn interest to build up the fund. To build up the fund, people who retired before 1940 received only one lump sum payment rather than monthly benefits.

1. Which program was funded by taxes on employers?

   _____

2. Which program was not administered by the states?

   _____

3. Which of these six programs do you think was the best? Why?

   _____

   _____

   _____

4. Do you think it's right for people working today to pay extra taxes to support workers who have retired? Why or why not?

   _____

   _____

   _____

Name: _____ Date: _____

What If?

1. What if you had been a child during the Great Depression? What could you have done to help your family get through the bad times?

    _____

    _____

    _____

    _____

    _____

2. What if you had been elected president in 1932 during the Great Depression? What would your priorities have been? What types of laws would you have wanted to pass first?

    _____

    _____

    _____

    _____

    _____

3. Write a "what if?" question about the Roaring Twenties or Great Depression and answer it.

    Question: _____

    _____

    _____

    Answer: _____

    _____

    _____

    _____

    _____

Name: _____ Date: _____

The Dust Bowl

Life had always been difficult for homesteaders on the Great Plains. Farms were small and water scarce with no reservoirs or irrigation systems. Even in good years, many were lucky to break even.

Before farmers moved to the area in the late 1800s, the land was covered with hardy grasses that held the fine-grained soil in place even during times of drought, wind, or torrential rains.

When large numbers of homesteaders settled in the region, they plowed up the grasses and planted crops. The cattle they raised ate whatever grass was left. This exposed the soil to the winds that constantly swept across the flat plains. When a series of droughts hit the area in the early thirties, combined with the farming practices of the past 50 years, there was nothing to hold the soil in place.

A large area in the southern part of the Great Plains region of the United States came to be known as the **Dust Bowl** during the 1930s. Much of this area suffered extensively from soil erosion.

The Depression had already caused the price of wheat and corn to fall to all-time lows. When crops failed, farmers couldn't make mortgage payments on their farms. By 1932, a thousand families a week were losing their farms in Texas, Oklahoma, and Arkansas. Thousands of families migrated west in search of a better life.

In 1935, both the federal and state governments began developing programs to conserve the soil and reclaim the area. This included seeding large areas with grass; the rotation of wheat, then sorghum, and then lying fallow; contour plowing; terracing; and strip planting. In some areas, "shelter belts" of trees were planted to break the force of the wind.

Use a dictionary to define these words.

1. reservoir: _____

2. irrigation: _____

3. erosion: _____

4. drought: _____

5. Learn more about one of the methods for conserving the soil or reclaiming the land listed in the previous paragraph. On your own paper, explain how it works and how it can help prevent soil loss.

Name: _____ Date: _____

Conditions Get Worse

The problems in the Dust Bowl area increased in 1936 when the winds began blowing almost continuously. People fled to shelter as huge clouds of dust advanced on them. Dust was carried great distances by the wind, in some cases darkening the sky all the way to the Atlantic Ocean.

During the next four years, as much as three to four inches of topsoil blew away, leaving only hard, red clay, which made farming impossible. Sand settled around homes, fences, and barns. People slept with wet cloths over their faces to filter out the dust. They woke to find themselves, their pillows, and blankets caked with dirt. Animals were buried alive or choked to death on the dust.

People died if they remained outside too long during a dust storm. Many also died from what came to be called "dust pneumonia"—severe damage to the lungs caused by breathing dust.

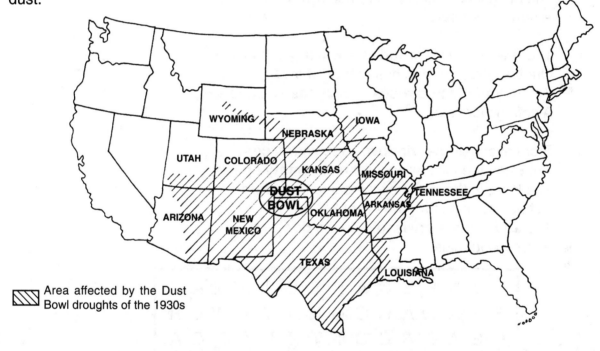

Area affected by the Dust Bowl droughts of the 1930s

1. Centered in northern Texas, the panhandle of Oklahoma, and southwestern Kansas, the Dust Bowl also included all or part of which other states?

_____

_____

_____

2. Which three states in the area affected by the Dust Bowl were farthest north?

_____

3. Which four states were completely in the area affected by the Dust Bowl?

_____

Name: _____ Date: _____

A Cottage for Sale

Music in the thirties reflected both pessimism due to economic conditions and optimism for a better time to come. People listened to upbeat songs like "Bye, Bye Blues," "Sunny Side Up," and "Get Happy" as well as songs with more serious themes, like "Brother, Can You Spare a Dime?"

Words from **"A Cottage for Sale"** recorded by Guy Lombardo in 1930 can be found in the puzzle. (At that time a cottage meant a small house, not a vacation place.) Look up, down, backward, forward, and diagonally to find and circle the words printed in bold.

Our **little dream castle** with **every** dream **gone**,
is **lonely and silent**, the **shades** are all **drawn**,
and my **heart** is **heavy** as I **gaze upon**
A **cottage** for **sale**.

The **lawn** we were **proud** of is **waving** in **hay**,
Our **beautiful garden** has **withered away**,
Where **you planted roses**, the **weeds seem** to **say**,
A cottage for sale.

From every **single window**, I **see** your **face**,
But when I reach a window, there's **empty space**,
The key's in the **mail** box the same as **before**,
But no one is **waiting any more**,
The **end** of the **story** is **told** on the **door**,
A cottage for sale.

```
B Y N F E C A P S L I A M A D
E E A W A N O G N I V A W E R
F S A S A C O T T Z E A T E A
O A T U S L E G T R Y N Z Y W
R L I T T L E D D A A A L V N
E E L G N I S K E L G E Y A H
S E S O R T F D P R N E H E W
H T V O N O P U J O E S N H O
A Z O E R O M O L Y E H D D D
D D L R R G A R D E N L T N N
E I U O Y Y T P M E O A A I I
S D E E W V W A I T I N G U W
```

Name: _____   Date: _____

Review of the Thirties

Match the definition in the right column with the corresponding term in the left column.

_____ 1. reservoir

A. Provided jobs for young, unemployed single men

_____ 2. erosion

B. A system used to carry water to where it is needed for crops

_____ 3. bankruptcy

C. A long period of time with little or no rain

_____ 4. Social Security Act

D. A place to hold surplus water for later use

_____ 5. Lame Duck Amendment

E. Broke; having no money; unable to pay debts

_____ 6. irrigation

F. Provided Old-Age Benefits

_____ 7. drought

G. Wearing away of soil due to wind or rain

_____ 8. Civilian Conservation Corps

H. Changed date of presidential inauguration

Circle "T" for True or "F" for False.

9. T F Isolationism is a disease that causes people to sleep a lot.

10. T F Franklin D. Roosevelt was elected president four times.

11. T F The thirties were called the Great Depression Era because most people were sad during those years.

12. T F The Dust Bowl was an annual football game played between the top two college teams in Texas.

13. T F Franklin D. Roosevelt was a Democrat.

14. T F During the Depression, people were often hungry. To show they had no food, they put empty bowls on the table and called them Dust Bowls.

15. T F Many flourishing cities were named Hooverville or Hoovertown in honor of Herbert Hoover.

16. T F Many of Roosevelt's New Deal programs were aimed at helping those who were unemployed.

17. T F MONOPOLY™ was invented by a rich businessman.

18. T F Radio brought music, news, weather, sports, dramas, comedies, and soap operas into millions of homes during the Depression.

Name: _____ Date: _____

Then and Now

Read the statements about conditions during the Great Depression. Add a statement about conditions today.

1. **Then:** Millions of people were unemployed.

    Now: _____

    _____

    _____

2. **Then:** Millions of people were homeless.

    Now: _____

    _____

    _____

3. **Then:** Listening to the radio and going to the movies were favorite pastimes.

    Now: _____

    _____

    _____

4. **Then:** MONOPOLY™ and Scrabble™ were popular board games. Children enjoyed play-ing with dolls, toy cars, blocks, and toy planes.

    Now: _____

    _____

    _____

5. **Then:** People enjoyed listening to jazz and dancing to Big Band music.

    Now: _____

    _____

    _____

6. **Then:** Franklin D. Roosevelt was president.

    Now: _____

    _____

    _____

Name: _____ Date: _____

What Else Happened Then?

Use reference sources to find one historical event for each year that occurred in the United States during the 1930s that was unrelated to the Great Depression or the Dust Bowl.

1930: _____

_____

_____

1931: _____

_____

_____

1932: _____

_____

_____

1933: _____

_____

_____

1934: _____

_____

_____

1935: _____

_____

_____

1936: _____

_____

_____

1937: _____

_____

_____

1938: _____

_____

_____

1939: _____

_____

_____

Name: _____ Date: _____

Read All About It!

Option 1: Read a fiction or nonfiction book about the Roaring Twenties or Great Depression.
Option 2: Read a biography of someone who played a role in history at that time.
Option 3: Read one of the books that received the Newberry Award between 1922 and 1939. (See the book list on the following page.)

Title and author of the book: _____

_____

Was the book fiction or nonfiction? _____

What years were covered in the book? _____

Briefly describe the main character. _____

_____

_____

Where did the main character live? _____

Summarize two major events described in the book. _____

_____

_____

_____

_____

What was the major problem the main character had to face? _____

_____

_____

How was that problem resolved? If it wasn't resolved, why not? _____

_____

_____

_____

Did you like the book? Why or why not? _____

_____

Newberry Award Winners

1939 Winner: *Thimble Summer* by Elizabeth Enright
      Honor Books: *Nino* by Valenti Angelo
                    Mr. Popper's Penguins by Richard & Florence Atwater
1938 Winner: *The White Stag* by Kate Seredy
      Honor Books: *Pecos Bill* by James Cloyd Bowman
                    On the Banks of Plum Creek by Laura Ingalls Wilder
1937 Winner: *Roller Skates* by Ruth Sawyer
      Honor Books: *Phoebe Fairchild: Her Book* by Lois Lenski
                    Whistler's Van by Idwal Jones
1936 Winner: *Caddie Woodlawn* by Carol Ryrie Brink
      Honor Books: *Honk, the Moose* by Phil Stong
                    The Good Master by Kate Seredy
1935 Winner: *Dobry* by Monica Shannon
      Honor Books: *Davy Crockett* by Constance Rourke
                    Pageant of Chinese History by Elizabeth Seeger
1934 Winner: *Invincible Louisa: The Story of the Author of Little Women* by Cornelia Meigs
      Honor Books: *Swords of Steel* by Elsie Singmaster
                    The Forgotten Daughter by Caroline Snedeker
1933 Winner: *Young Fu of the Upper Yangtze* by Elizabeth Lewis
      Honor Books: *The Railroad to Freedom: A Story of the Civil War* by Hildegarde Swift
                    Swift Rivers by Cornelia Meigs
1932 Winner: *Waterless Mountain* by Laura Adams Armer
      Honor Books: *The Fairy Circus* by Dorothy P. Lathrop
                    Calico Bush by Rachel Field
1931 Winner: *The Cat Who Went to Heaven* by Elizabeth Coatsworth
      Honor Books: *Floating Island* by Anne Parrish
                    Spice and the Devil's Cave by Agnes Hewes
1930 Winner: *Hitty: Her First Hundred Years* by Rachel Field
      Honor Books: *The Tangle-Coated Horse and Other Tales* by Ella Young
                    Pran of Albania by Elizabeth Miller
1929 Winner: *The Trumpeter of Krakow* by Eric P. Kelly
      Honor Books: *Pigtail of Ah Lee Ben Loo* by John Bennett
                    Millions of Cats by Wanda Gag
1928 Winner: *Gay-Neck: The Story of a Pigeon* by Dhan Gopal Mukerji
      Honor Books: *The Wonder Smith and His Son* by Ella Young
                    Downright Dencey by Caroline Snedeker
1927 Winner: *Smoky, the Cowhorse* by Will James
1926 Winner: *Shen of the Sea* by Arthur Bowie Chrisman
1925 Winner: *Tales from Silver Lands* by Charles J. Finger
1924 Winner: *The Dark Frigate* by Charles B. Hawes
1923 Winner: *The Voyages of Doctor Dolittle* by Hugh Lofting
1922 Winner: *The Story of Mankind* by Hendrik Willem Van Loon

History Projects

Complete one of these projects. Work alone, with a partner, or with a small group if appropriate.

- Create a detailed time line of the Roaring Twenties or Great Depression with illustrations and maps.

- Make a videotape of an interview with a bootlegger.

- Write and perform a short play about conditions in a Hooverville.

- Do a detailed comparison between any two of the men who were president in the 1920s and/or 1930s. Include ways they were alike and ways they were different.

- Make a scrapbook about the Roaring Twenties. Add captions for all pictures. You can download pictures from the Internet, photocopy them from books, or draw your own.

- Write articles for one page of a newspaper dated any time between 1920 and 1935.

- Write and illustrate a poem about the Roaring Twenties. Read your poem to the group.

- Make a model of a biplane and explain how it worked.

- Learn and demonstrate a dance popular in the Roaring Twenties, like the Charleston or the Lindy Hop. Teach others to do the dance.

- Write a detailed report about the conditions in your city or community during the Great Depression. Include copies of local newspaper articles.

- Create a journal that could have been written by someone between 1929 and 1935 describing everyday life and events. Include at least five entries for each year.

- Prepare and present a ten-minute speech either in favor of or against Prohibition.

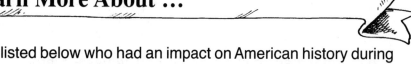

Learn More About …

Learn more about one of the people listed below who had an impact on American history during the Roaring Twenties and/or the Great Depression Era. Use the Internet and other reference sources to write a three- to five-page report with illustrations.

Charles Lindbergh

Amelia Earhart

Marian Anderson
Louis Armstrong
Pearl S. Buck
Richard Byrd
Al Capone
Charlie Chaplin
Calvin Coolidge
Douglas Corrigan
Charles Coughlin
Walt Disney
Isadora Duncan
Amelia Earhart
Duke Ellington
Edna Ferber
Henry Ford
George Gershwin
Benny Goodman
Woody Guthrie
Warren G. Harding
Ernest Hemingway
Herbert Hoover

Harry Houdini
Sinclair Lewis
Charles Lindbergh
Huey Long
Amy Lowell
Margaret Mead
Jelly Roll Morton
Jesse Owens
Frances Perkins
Will Rogers
Eleanor Roosevelt
Franklin D. Roosevelt
Nellie Tayloe Ross
Florence Sabin
Margaret Sanger
Upton Sinclair
Bessie Smith
Gertrude Stein
John Steinbeck
Francis Townsend
Rudolph Valentino

Walt Disney

Rudolph Valentino

Isadora Duncan

Suggested Reading

The Noble Experiment, 1919–1933 by James P. Barry

Ticket to the Twenties: A Time Traveler's Guide by Mary Blocksma

Herbert Hoover by Susan Clinton

The Great Depression by David Downing

The Lindbergh Baby Kidnapping in American History by Judith Edwards

War, Peace, and All that Jazz by Joy Hakim

The Scopes Monkey Trial: A Headline Court Case by Freya Hanson

The Story of the Teapot Dome Scandal by Jim Hardgrove

An Album of the Great Depression by William Loren Katz

Calvin Coolidge by Zachary Kent

Life During the Great Depression by Dennis Nishi

Franklin D. Roosevelt by Alice Osinksi

Children of the Dust Bowl: The True Story of the School at Weedpatch Camp by Jerry Stanley

The Roaring Twenties by R. Conrad Stein

The Story of the Great Depression by R. Conrad Stein

Timelines: 1920s by Gail B. Stewart

Timelines: 1930s by Gail B. Stewart

The 1930s: Picture History of the 20th Century by Richard Tames

The Teapot Dome Scandal: A Headline Court Case by Jonathan L. Thorndike

The Thirties: An Illustrated History in Colour 1930–1939 by J. Unstead

The Twenties: An Illustrated History in Colour 1919–1929 by J. Unstead

Warren G. Harding by Linda R. Wade

The LIFE History of the United States: Volumes 10 and 11.

Answer Keys

Women Finally Allowed to Vote (p. 7)
1. Wyoming in 1869
2. and 3. Answers will vary. See map.
4. With the exception of New York, none of the eastern or southern states had allowed full suffrage before the Nineteenth Amendment was passed. The states that did were all west of the Mississippi River.

Louis Armstrong: Master of Improvisation (p. 12)
1. Improvise: to make up something as you go along
2. Ensemble: a group, usually of musicians
3. "Hello, Dolly"
4. Satchmo: also Dippermouth, Satchelmouth, and Pops

Meet John Calvin Coolidge (p. 13)
1. and 2. Answers will vary.
3. July 4, 1872, in Plymouth Notch, Vermont
4. Silent Cal
5. Republican
6. Lawyer
7. "Keep Cool with Coolidge"

What Could You Buy for a Dollar? (p. 16)
1. 27
2. Yes; you would have enough left to go to three movies.
3. 20　　4. 14　　5. $1.00

Learning a New Language: Jive Talk (p. 17)
1. B　2. M　3. H　4. F　5. L　6. R
7. A　8. G　9. N　10. C　11. O　12. Q
13. E　14. P　15. D　16. K　17. I　18. J

Twenties Scavenger Hunt (p. 18)
1. The Green Bay Packers
2. Chicago Bears
3. balloon tires
4. a dog
5. The Harlem Globetrotters
6. Margaret Gorman of Washington, D.C.
7. Nellie Tayloe Ross
8. *The Spirit of St. Louis*
9. 33 hours and 32 minutes
10. Alexander Fleming

Up, Up, and Away (p. 19)
1. O　2. F　3. F　4. O
5. F　6. O　7. F　8. O

Who's Who? (p. 20)
1. singer (opera)　　2. (jazz) musician
3. dancer/actor　　4. author
5. actor　　6. pilot
7. boxer　　8. film maker
9. pilot　　10. composer
11. (jazz) musician　　12. football player
13. actress　　14. magician
15. golfer　　16. boxer
17. anthropologist　　18. (jazz) musician
19. Olympic medal winner (track)
20. baseball player　　21. (jazz) singer
22. author　　23. tennis player
24. boxer
25. Olympic medal winner (swimmer)/actor

The Other Side of the Coin (p. 22)
All would be Then & Now except playing video games, watching television, and riding skateboards, which would be Now Only.

Review the Twenties (p. 24)
1. C　2. H　3. A　4. F　5. G　6. D
7. J　8. I　9. E　10. B　11. F　12. T
13. F　14. T　15. T　16. F　17. T　18. F
19. F　20. F

The Crash Heard Around the World (p. 26)
2. Depression: a time when prices are high and wages, low; often marked by periods of high unemployment

The 1930s (p. 27)
1. Bankruptcy: broke; having no money; being unable to pay one's debts

Meet Young Franklin D. Roosevelt (p. 30)
1. James M. Cox

The Lame Duck Amendment (p. 34)
1. They wanted to decrease the time between the election and when the officials took office.
2. A "lame duck" was considered helpless or ineffective. Someone who had not been reelected was often helpless to get anything done in the time after the election until his term ended.
3. Answers will vary.
4. There must be a clear line of people who are qualified to take over the presidency so that the government can continue smoothly even in a crisis situation.

Math Facts (p. 35)
1. $24
2. $1,248
3. Answer will depend on current year.
4. 4,726 miles
5. 7 hours
6. $0.50 per hour
7. $169
8. $15
9. $360
10. 36%
11. 15,856,593
12. 17,064,426

What Happened When? (p. 38)
1. 1932 in Lake Placid, New York
2. *LIFE* and *Look*
3. *Snow White and the Seven Dwarfs*
4. Franklin D. Roosevelt
5. 1931
6. Half
7. Empire State Building
8. Cost rose from 2 cents to 3 cents
9. Frances Perkins
10. 13 million
11. 40 cents an hour
12. Twenty-First
13. 1935
14. electric typewriters
15. *Funnies on Parade*

New Deal Programs (p. 40)
2. The workers built roads and hiking trails, cleaned beaches, cleared camping sites, laid telephone lines, built fire observation towers, and planted trees. These projects benefitted the public.

Desperate Times, Desperate People, Desperate Actions (p. 41)
1. It got rid of the Association's surplus of apples, made apples available to the consumers, and gave the unemployed a source of income.

An Alphabet Soup of New Deal Programs (p. 42)
1. Federal Deposit Insurance Corporation
2. Tennessee Valley Authority
3. Federal Emergency Relief Administration
4. Agricultural Adjustment Act
5. Home Owners' Loan Corporation
6. National Recovery Administration

Let's Listen to the Radio (p. 43)
1. Music, news, weather, sports, advertisements, comedies, dramas
2. Television
3. The actors had to look the part for their characters in television and movies.

Meet Eleanor Roosevelt (p. 44)
1. mother, maternal grandmother
2. ten
3. England
4. Franklin Roosevelt
5. My Day
6. Boulder (Hoover)

7. Lincoln Memorial
8. United Nations
9. Roosevelt
10. former U.S. President, Theodore Roosevelt

Thirties Scavenger Hunt (p. 47)
1. Kaw
2. Babe Ruth
3. Ronald Reagan
4. tax evasion
5. The "William Tell Overture"
6. Jay Silverheels
7. Gene Autry
8. Band leader
9. Abraham Isaac Arshawasky

The Social Security Act of 1935 (p. 48)
1. Unemployment Compensation
2. Old-Age Benefits (Social Security)

The Dust Bowl (p. 50)
1. Reservoir: a place to hold water for later use
2. Irrigation: a system used to carry water to where it is needed
3. Erosion: wearing away of soil due to wind or rain
4. Drought: period of little or no rain

Conditions Get Worse (p. 51)
1. Utah, Arizona, New Mexico, Colorado, Wyoming, Nebraska, Kansas, Iowa, Missouri, Tennessee, Arkansas, Nevada, and Louisiana
2. Wyoming, Nebraska, and Iowa
3. New Mexico, Texas, Oklahoma, and Kansas

A Cottage for Sale (p. 52)

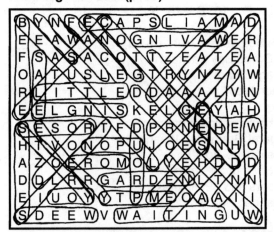

Review of the Thirties (p. 53)
1. D
2. G
3. E
4. F
5. H
6. B
7. C
8. A
9. F
10. T
11. F
12. F
13. T
14. F
15. F
16. T
17. F
18. T